HOT METAL Vol. II

Music Engraving by W.R. Music
Production Manager: Daniel Rosenbaum
Art Direction: Alisa Hill
Administration: Tom Haydock
Director of Music: Mark Phillips

ISBN: 0-89524-439-X

COVER PHOTOS:

Guns N' Roses - Neil Zlozower
Van Halen - Alberto Tolot
Metallica - Ross Halfin
Tesla - Neil Zlozower
Vinnie Vincent Invasion - Mark Weiss
Faster Pussycat - Jay David Buchsbaum

ALPHABETICAL CONTENTS

CONTENTS

TABLATURE EXPLANATION

TABLATURE A six-line staff that graphically represents the guitar fingerboard. By placing a number on the appropriate line, the string and fret of any note can be indicated. For example:

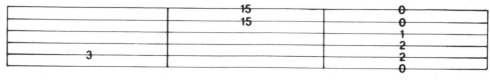

5th string, 3rd fret   *1st string, 15th fret,*   *an open E chord*
2nd string, 15th fret,
played together

Definitions for Special Guitar Notation (For both traditional and tablature guitar lines)

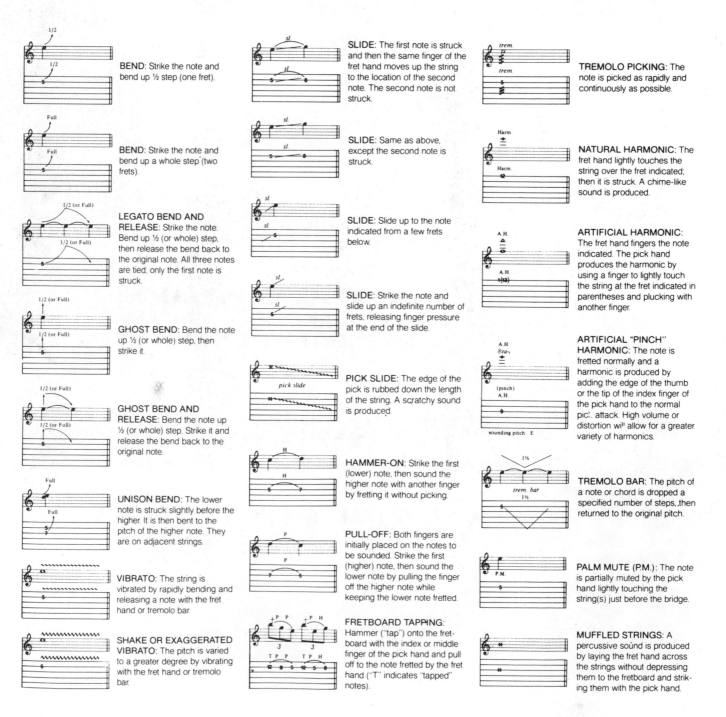

BEND: Strike the note and bend up ½ step (one fret).

BEND: Strike the note and bend up a whole step (two frets).

LEGATO BEND AND RELEASE: Strike the note. Bend up ½ (or whole) step, then release the bend back to the original note. All three notes are tied; only the first note is struck.

GHOST BEND: Bend the note up ½ (or whole) step, then strike it.

GHOST BEND AND RELEASE: Bend the note up ½ (or whole) step. Strike it and release the bend back to the original note.

UNISON BEND: The lower note is struck slightly before the higher. It is then bent to the pitch of the higher note. They are on adjacent strings.

VIBRATO: The string is vibrated by rapidly bending and releasing a note with the fret hand or tremolo bar.

SHAKE OR EXAGGERATED VIBRATO: The pitch is varied to a greater degree by vibrating with the fret hand or tremolo bar.

SLIDE: The first note is struck and then the same finger of the fret hand moves up the string to the location of the second note. The second note is not struck.

SLIDE: Same as above, except the second note is struck.

SLIDE: Slide up to the note indicated from a few frets below.

SLIDE: Strike the note and slide up an indefinite number of frets, releasing finger pressure at the end of the slide.

PICK SLIDE: The edge of the pick is rubbed down the length of the string. A scratchy sound is produced.

HAMMER-ON: Strike the first (lower) note, then sound the higher note with another finger by fretting it without picking.

PULL-OFF: Both fingers are initially placed on the notes to be sounded. Strike the first (higher) note, then sound the lower note by pulling the finger off the higher note while keeping the lower note fretted.

FRETBOARD TAPPING: Hammer ("tap") onto the fretboard with the index or middle finger of the pick hand and pull off to the note fretted by the fret hand ("T" indicates "tapped" notes).

TREMOLO PICKING: The note is picked as rapidly and continuously as possible.

NATURAL HARMONIC: The fret hand lightly touches the string over the fret indicated; then it is struck. A chime-like sound is produced.

ARTIFICIAL HARMONIC: The fret hand fingers the note indicated. The pick hand produces the harmonic by using a finger to lightly touch the string at the fret indicated in parentheses and plucking with another finger.

ARTIFICIAL "PINCH" HARMONIC: The note is fretted normally and a harmonic is produced by adding the edge of the thumb or the tip of the index finger of the pick hand to the normal pick attack. High volume or distortion will allow for a greater variety of harmonics.

TREMOLO BAR: The pitch of a note or chord is dropped a specified number of steps, then returned to the original pitch.

PALM MUTE (P.M.): The note is partially muted by the pick hand lightly touching the string(s) just before the bridge.

MUFFLED STRINGS: A percussive sound is produced by laying the fret hand across the strings without depressing them to the fretboard and striking them with the pick hand.

GUNS N' ROSES

PARADISE CITY
As recorded by GUNS N' ROSES

Words and Music by
W. Axl Rose, Slash, Izzy Stradlin',
Duff "Rose" McKagan and Steven Adler

1. Just a ur-chin liv-in' un-der the street.__ I'm a ___ hard case that's tough to beat.__ I'm your
2.3.4. *See additional lyrics*

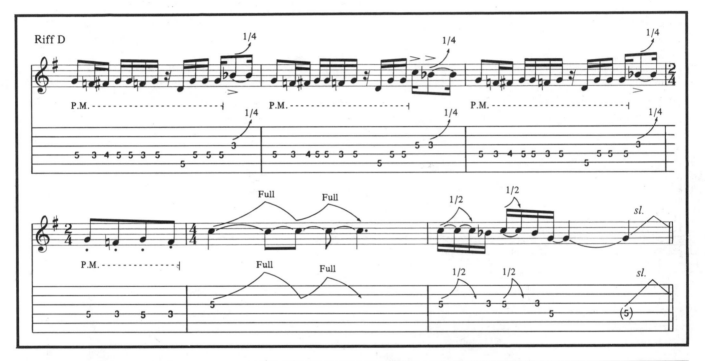

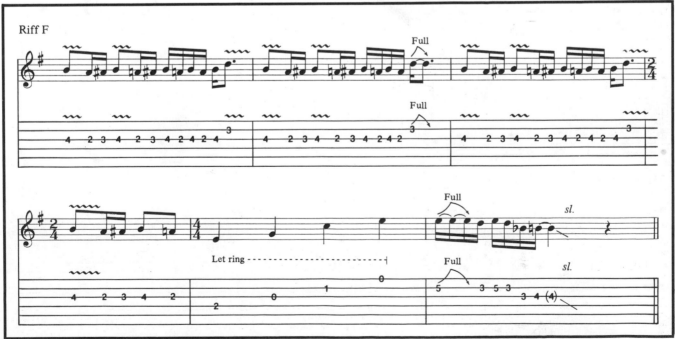

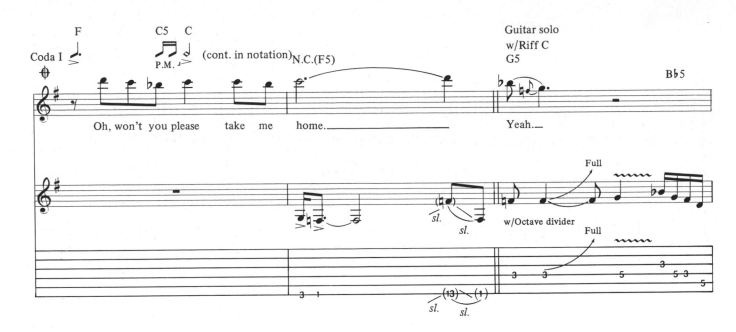

Oh, won't you please take me home._____ Yeah.—

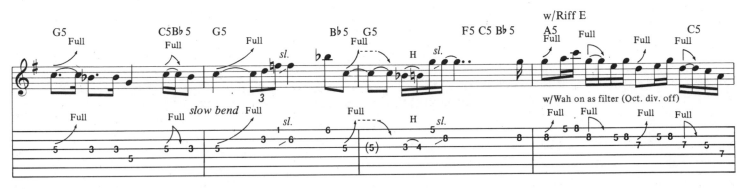

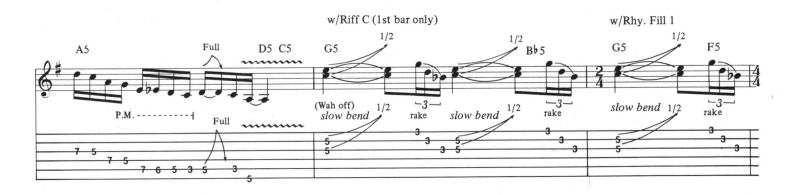

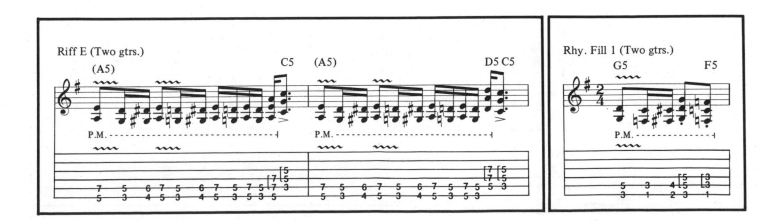

Oh, won't you please take me home,

home.

* Slow slide up middle 4 strings (off neck)

*As before

Double time ♩ = 208

Rhy.
Fig. 3

* Slow slide up middle 4 strings (off neck)

w/Lead vocal ad lib (on Chorus) *(till notation returns)*
*w/Rhy. Fig. 3 *(9½ times)*
**G5

w/Octave divider

*Vary strumming rhythm at will.

** Use "type 2" till end.

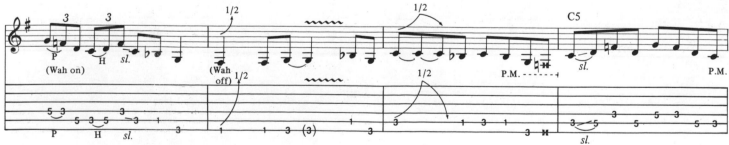

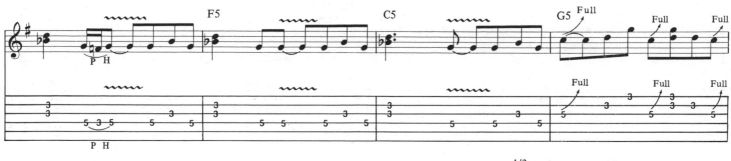

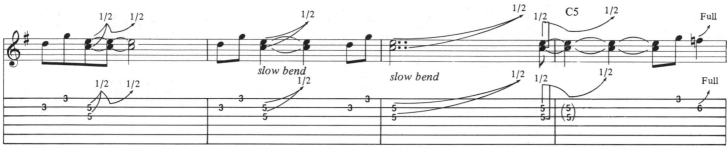

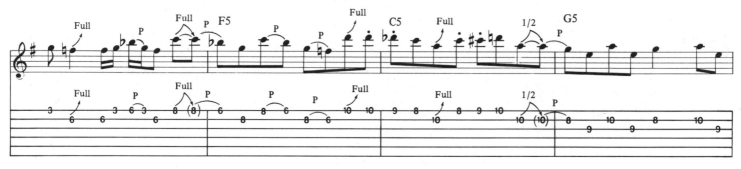

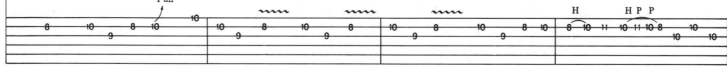

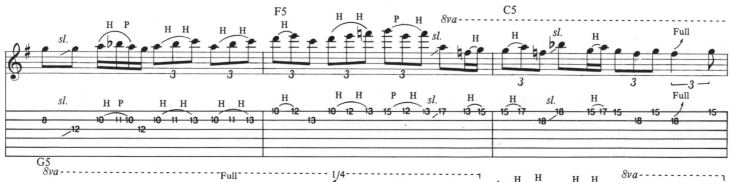

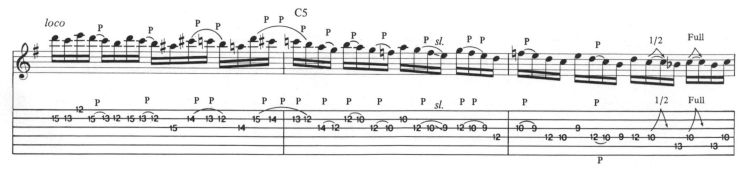

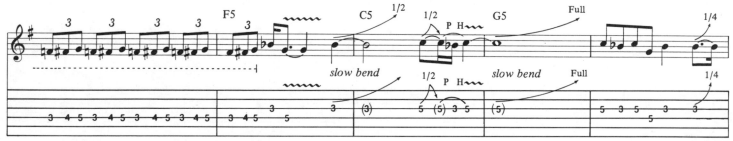

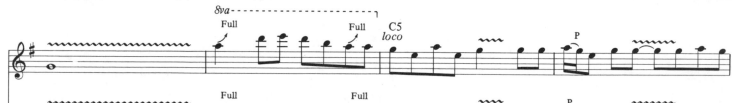

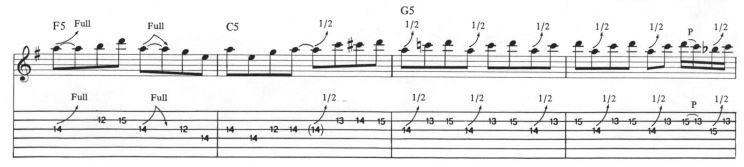

Additional Lyrics

2. Ragz to richez, or so they say.
    Ya gotta keep pushin' for the fortune and fame.
    It's all a gamble when it's just a game.
    Ya treat it like a capital crime.
    Everybody's doin' their time. *(To Chorus)*

3. Strapped in the chair of the city's gas chamber,
    Why I'm here I can't quite remember.
    The surgeon general says it's hazardous to breathe.
    I'd have another cigarette but I can't see.
    Tell me who ya gonna believe? *(To Chorus)*

4. Captain America's been torn a part.
    Now he's a court jester with a broken heart.
    He said, "Turn me around and take me back to the start."
    I must be losin' my mind. "Are you blind?"
    I've seen it all a million times. *(To Chorus)*

PATIENCE

As recorded by GUNS N' ROSES

Words and Music by
W. Axl Rose, Slash, Izzy Stradlin',
Duff "Rose" McKagan and Steven Adler

16

1. Shed a tear 'cause I'm miss - in'___ you,___ I'm still al - right___ to smile.___
2. *See additional lyrics*

Girl, I think a-bout___ you ev'-ry day___ now.

(end Rhy. Fig. 2)

(end Rhy. Fig.2A)

w/Rhy. Figs. 2 & 2A (both 1st 6 bars only)

Was a time when I was-n't___ sure___ but you set my mind___ at ease.___

w/Rhy. Fill 1

There is no doubt___you're in ___ my heart ___ now.

Rhy.
Fig. 3 Cadd9

Said, wom-an,___ take it slow,___ it'll work it-self___ out fine.___

Rhy. Fig. 3A
Gtr. II

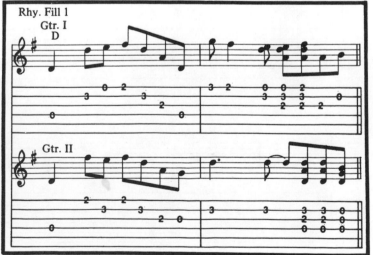

Rhy. Fill 1
Gtr. I

Gtr. II

18

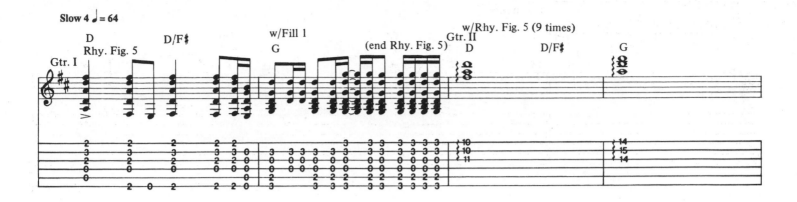

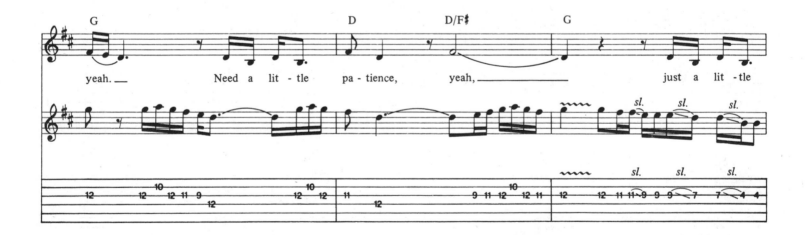

Additional Lyrics

2. I sit here on the stairs 'cause I'd rather be alone.
   If I can't have you right now I'll wait, dear.
   Sometimes I get so tense but I can't speed up the time.
   But you know, love, there's one more thing to consider.

   Said, woman, take it slow and things will be just fine.
   You and I'll just use a little patience.
   Said, sugar, take the time 'cause the lights are shining bright.
   You and I've got what it takes to make it.
   We won't fake it, ah, I'll never break it 'cause I can't take it. *(To Gtr. solo)*

Eika Aoshima

VAN HALEN

"5150"
As recorded by VAN HALEN

Words and Music by
Edward Van Halen, Sammy Hagar,
Michael Anthony and Alex Van Halen

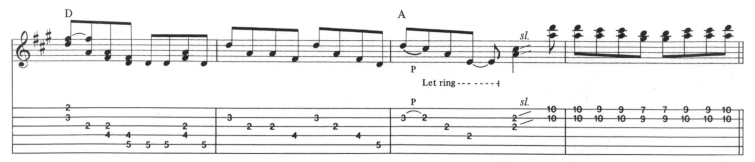

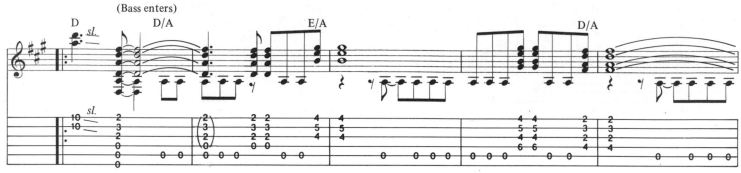

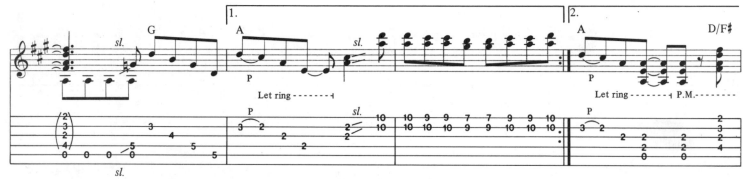

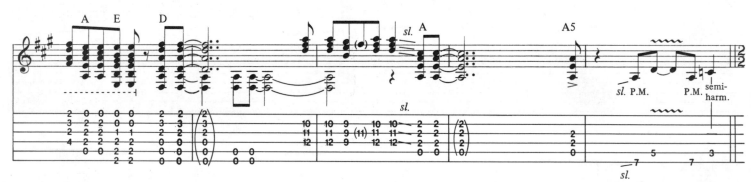

Half-time feel
1st, 2nd Verses

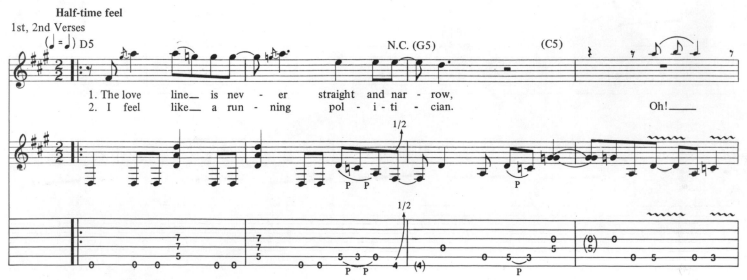

1. The love line_ is nev - er straight and nar - row,
2. I feel like_ a run - ning pol - i - ti - cian.

Oh!____

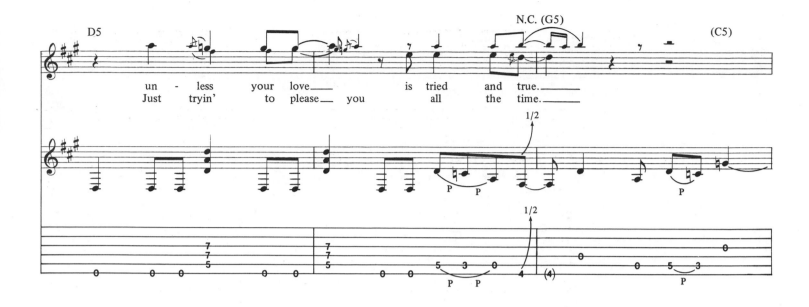

un - less   your   love____   is   tried   and   true.____
Just   tryin'   to   please____ you   all   the   time.____

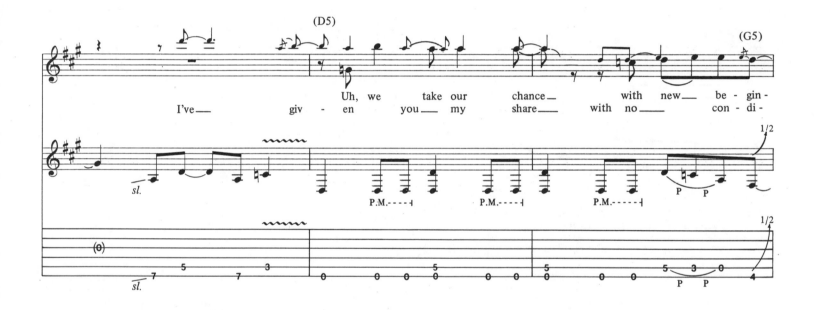

Uh, we   take   our   chance____   with   new____ be - gin -
I've____ giv - en   you____ my   share____ with   no____   con - di -

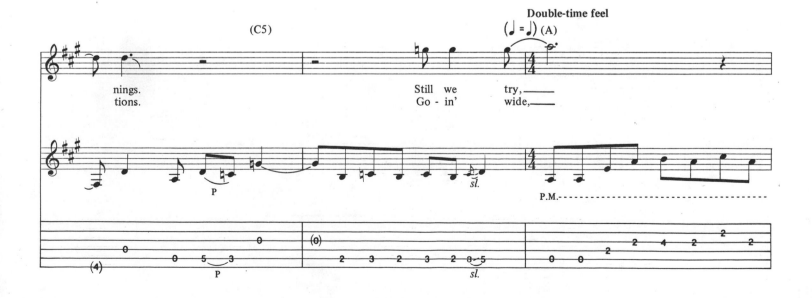

nings.   Still   we   try,____
tions.   Go - in'   wide,____

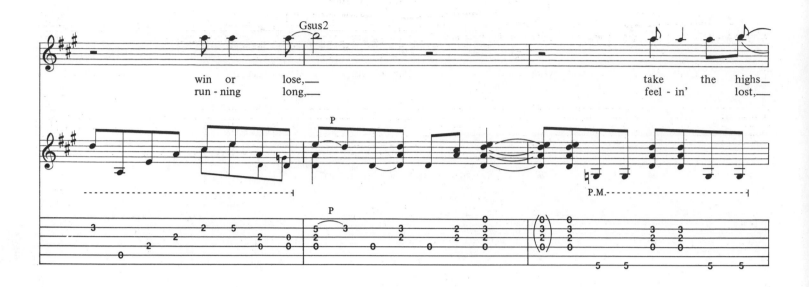

win or lose,___ take the highs___
run - ning long,___ feel - in' lost,___

with the blues.___
but not___ for long.___

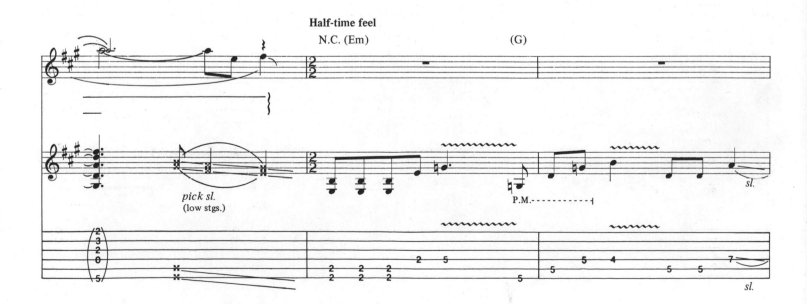

Guitar solo

*Push string against pick-up pole piece.

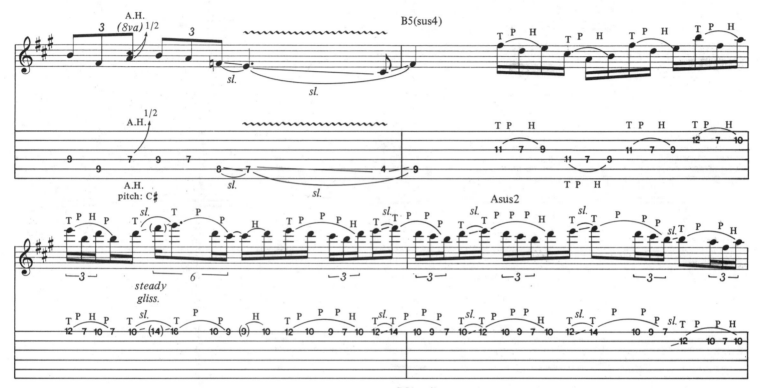

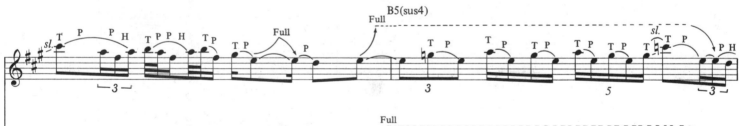

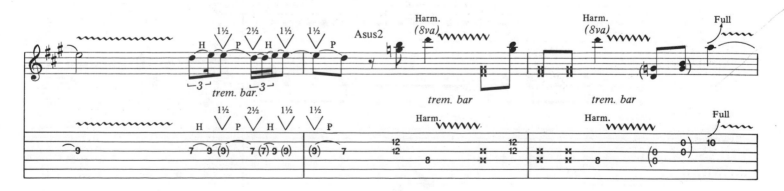

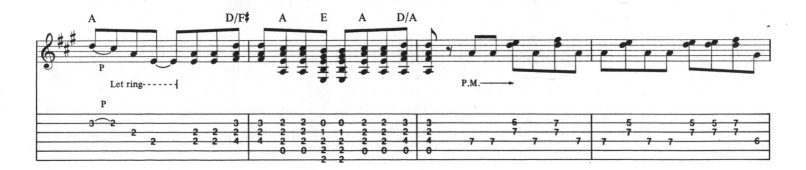

SOURCE OF INFECTION
As recorded by VAN HALEN

Words and Music by
Edward Van Halen, Sammy Hagar,
Michael Anthony and Alex Van Halen

40

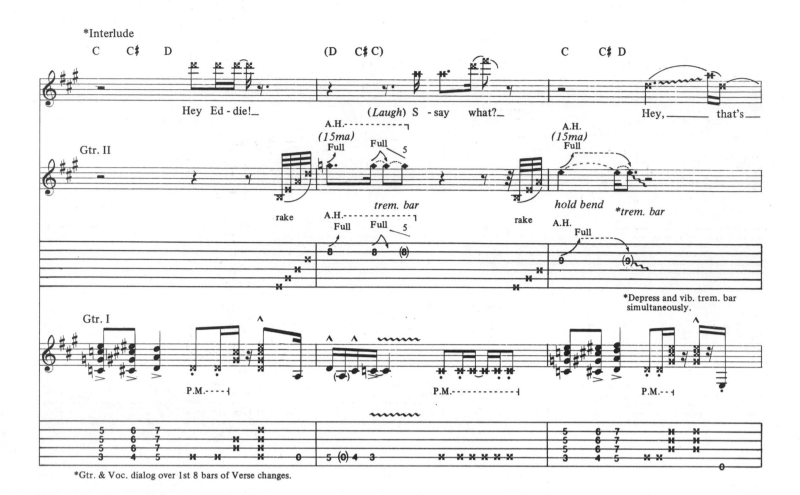

*Interlude

*Gtr. & Voc. dialog over 1st 8 bars of Verse changes.

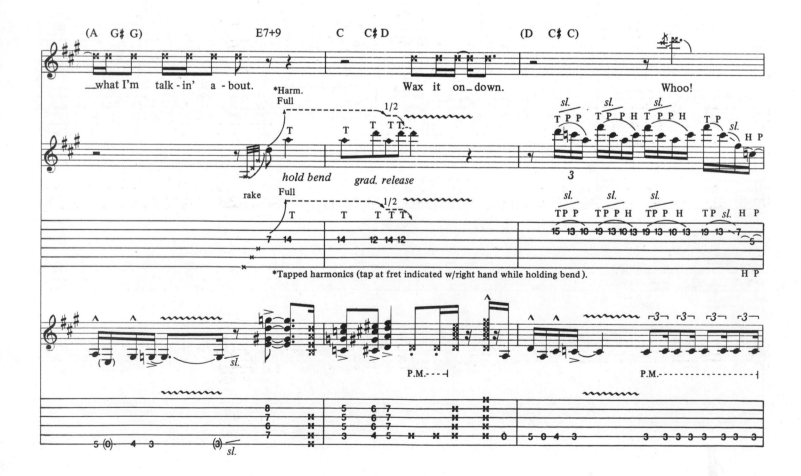

Rrr - read-y, set, go!

*String flab.

Guitar solo 1

Oh, yeah.

*Verse (2nd 8 bars) changes in F#minor implied by bass.

(Vocal: *Whoo!*)

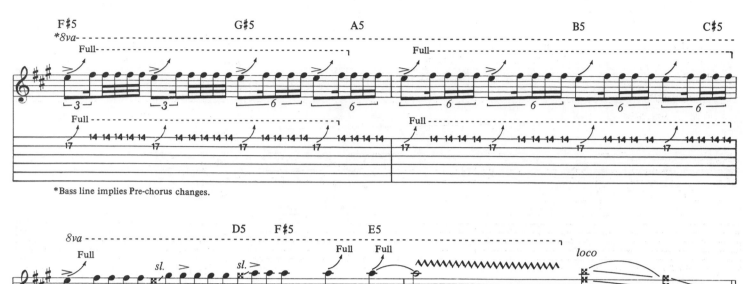

F#5   G#5   A5   B5   C#5

*Bass line implies Pre-chorus changes.

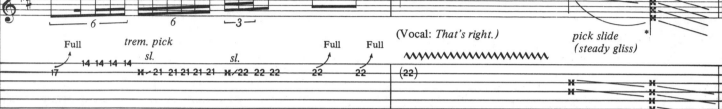

D5   F#5   E5

(Vocal: *That's right.*)

*Add left hand slide on
6 stg. on beat 4.

Chorus

A5/F#   B5/F#   A5/F#   E/F#   A5/F#   B5/F#

Love,_____   love is __ the __ source __   (of __ in -

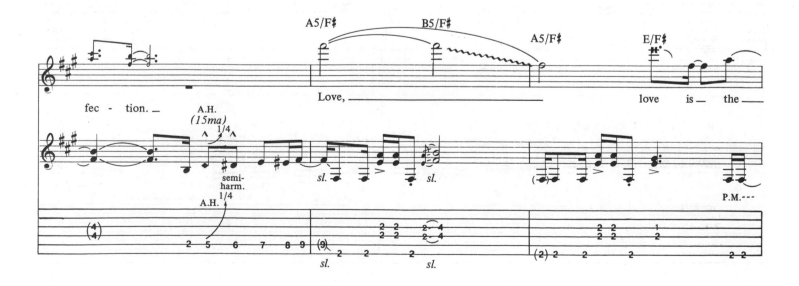

A5/F#   B5/F#   A5/F#   E/F#

fec - tion. __   Love,_____   love is __ the __

44

Ross Halfin

BLACKENED
As recorded by METALLICA

Words and Music by
James Hetfield, Lars Ulrich
and Jason Newsted

THE SHORTEST STRAW
As recorded by METALLICA

Words and Music by
James Hetfield and Lars Ulrich

1st, 2nd, 3rd Verses

Sus - pi - cion is your name. Your hon - es - ty to blame. Put dig - ni - ty to shame.
The ac - cu - sa - tions fly. Dis - crim - i - na - tion, why? Your in - ner self to die.
Be - hind you hands are tied. Your be - ing os - tra - cized. Your hell is mul - ti - plied.

Dis - hon - or. Witch - hunt, mod - ern day. De - ter - min - ing de - cay.
In - trud - ing. Doubt sunk it - self in you. Its teeth and tal - ons through.
Up - end - ing. The fall - out has be - gun. Op - pres - sive dam - age done.

The bla - tant dis - ar - ray. Dis - fig - ure. The pub - lic eye's dis - grace.
Your liv - ing catch two - two. De - lud - ing. A mass hys - ter - i - a.
Your man - y turn to none. To noth - ing. You're reach - ing your na - dir.

De - fy - ing com - mon place. Un - end - ing pa - per chase. Un - end - ing.
A meg - a - lo - man - i - a. Re - veal de - men - ti - a. Re - veal.
Your will has dis - ap - peared. The lie is crys - tal clear. De - fend - ing.

Deaf - en - ing. Pains - tak - ing. Reck - on - ing.
Se - cret - ly. Si - lent - ly. Cer - tain - ly.
Chan - nels red. One word said. Black - list - ed.

This ver - ti - go, it doth bring.
In ver - ti - go you will be.
With ver - ti - go make you dead.

57

Tempo I
w/Rhy. Fig. 1
E5 F5 E5 E
E5 F5 E5 G5 B♭5
F5 E5 E
E5 F5 E5 B♭5 G5
6 open
Pulled for you.
Pulled for
(Short - est straw.
Short - est straw.
F5 E5 E
E5 F5 E5 G5 B♭5
F5 E5 E
E5 F5 E5 G5 F♯5 F5
you.
Pulled for you.
Short - est straw has been pulled for you.
Short - est straw.
Short - est straw.)
1/2 Full
Full
P
H
1½
8va
loco
D.S. al Coda
sl.
*Vol. knob swell.
Coda
Pulled for you.
Double time feel
w/Riff A
E5 F5 D/F♯
G5 F♯5 F5
E5 F5 E5 F5 E5
rit.

NEIL ZLOZOWER

TE∫LA

CUMIN' ATCHA LIVE
As recorded by TESLA

Words and Music by
Jeffrey Keith, Frank Hannon
and Brian Wheat

Here I come, ____ cum - in' at - cha live. ____

Chorus

(Cum - in' at - cha live!)

Cum - in' at - cha live. ____

(Cum - in' at - cha live!)

Cum - in' at - cha live. ____

(Cum - in' at - cha live!)

Oh, here I

come. ____

Riff A   (Three gtrs.)

*All gtrs. vibrato.

(end Riff A)

(Drum fill)

slow bend

Lead gtr. I

loco

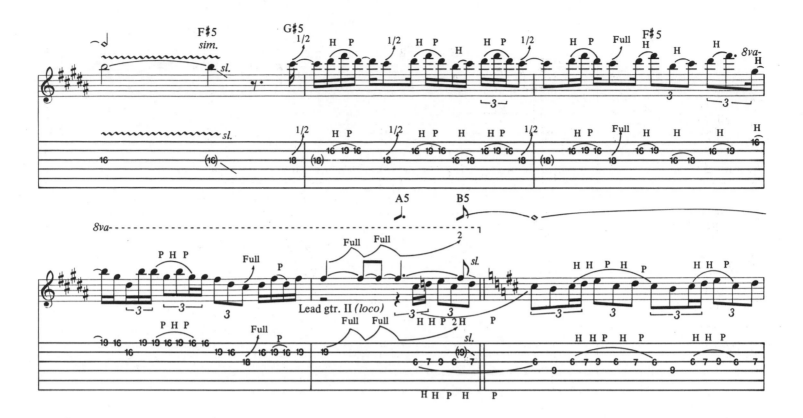

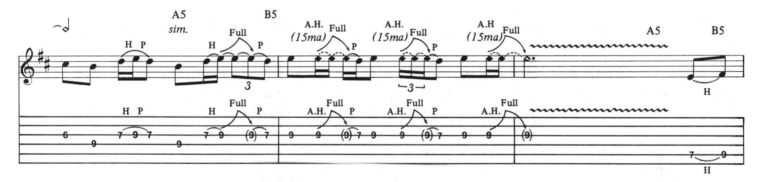

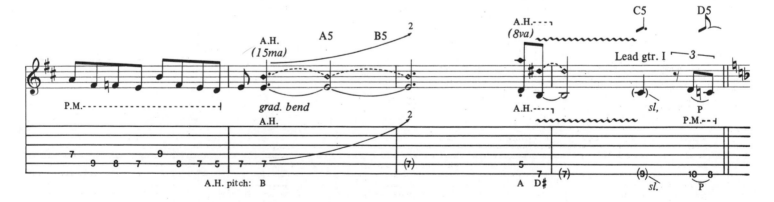

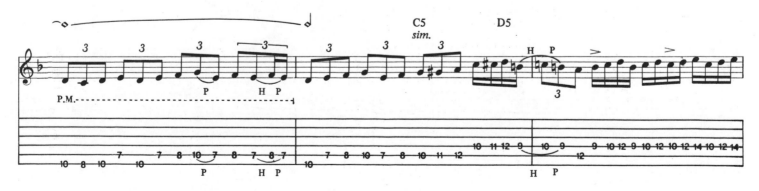

*Pull up on bar.

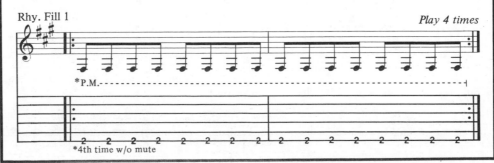

ROCK ME TO THE TOP

As recorded by TESLA

Words and Music by
Jeffrey Keith and Tommy Skeoch

Additional Lyrics

2. I take command, take control.
   Now I see you're comin' back for more.
   You say you like it but you need it.
   Ooh, you wanna feel it.
   I'm in the air, feel me surround you.
   Do anything that I want you to. Come on. *(To Chorus)*

William Hames

VINNIE VINCENT
INVASION

BREAKOUT

As recorded by VINNIE VINCENT INVASION

Words and Music by Vinnie Vincent

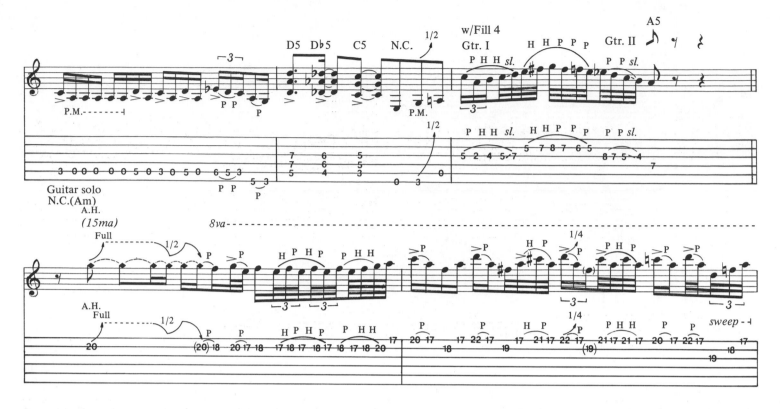

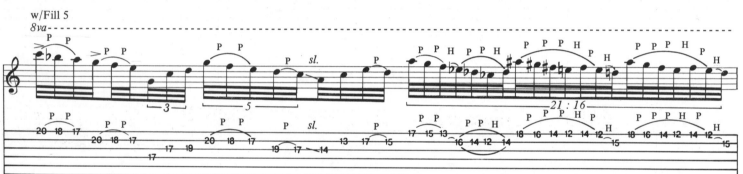

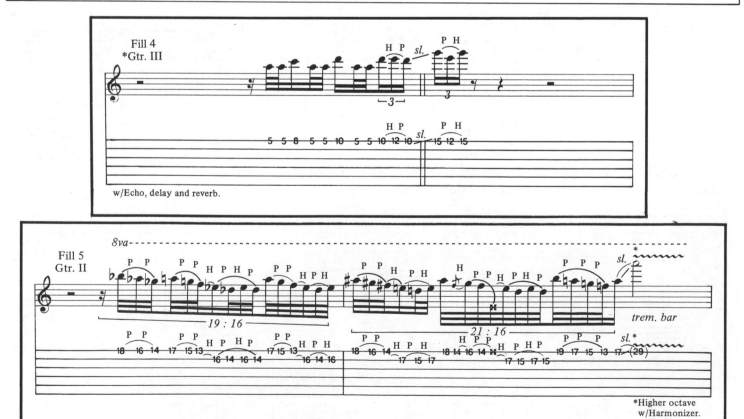

* Higher octave
w/Harmonizer.

* Gtr. IV is tuned down 1/2 step (Eb, Ab, Db, Gb, Bb, Eb)
and sounds 1/2 step lower than written.

Chorus
w/Rhy. Fig. 1

Free-dom calls me,— no chains can hold— me— down. ——— Rip it up,— we

w/Fill 6

make the laws and break it.— Sound of si-rens— wail-ing as the night cries.

Band of gyp-sies,— young— blood— on— the rise. ——————————— Oh, yeah!
(Break-out!)

SHOOT U FULL OF LOVE

As recorded by VINNIE VINCENT INVASION

Words and Music by Vinnie Vincent

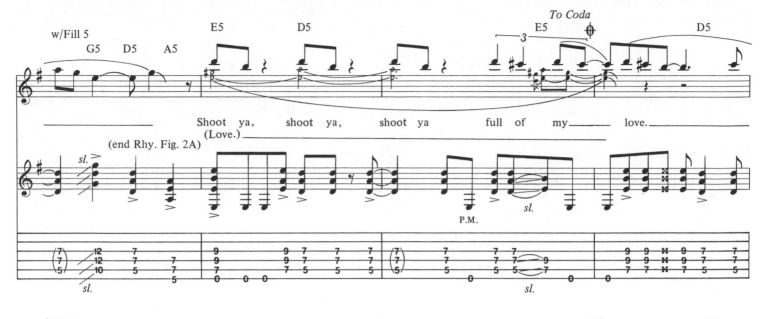

Shoot ya, shoot ya, shoot ya full of my___ love.___
(Love.)___

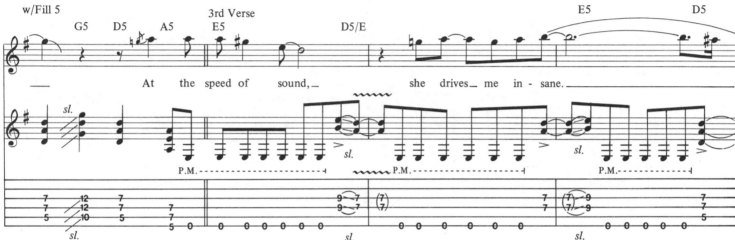

At the speed of sound,___ she drives___ me in - sane.

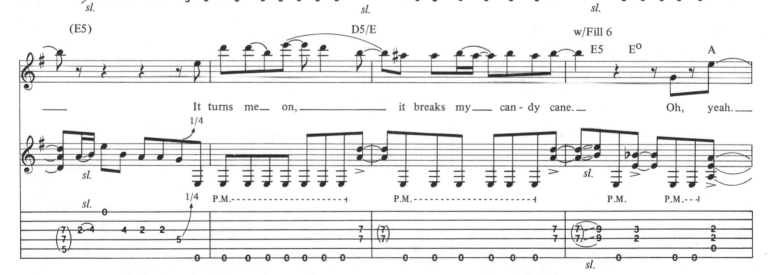

It turns me___ on,_____ it breaks my___ can - dy cane.___ Oh, yeah.___

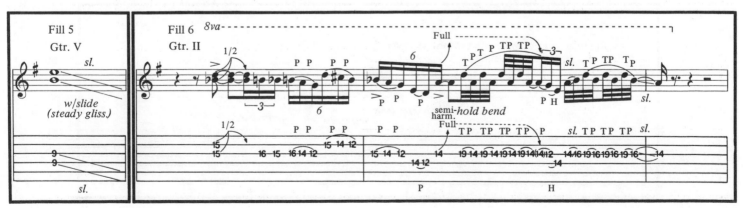

*Pull sharp with trem. bar

To -

night you're all I wan - na own. _____ Dis - con - nect my tel - e - phone! _

Shoot U full of _____ love. _____

Shoot U full of my love. _____

(Love.) _____

(Love.) _____

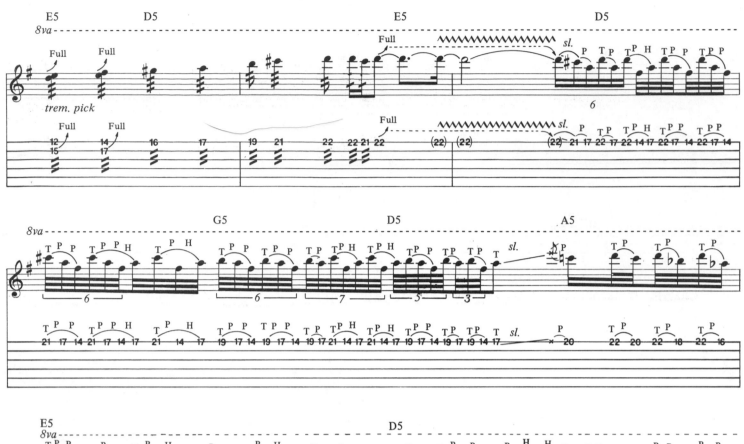

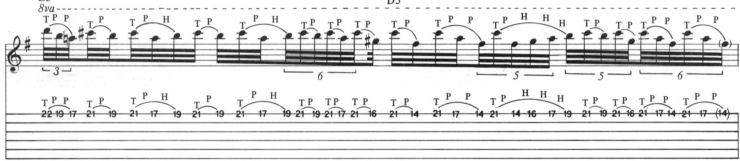

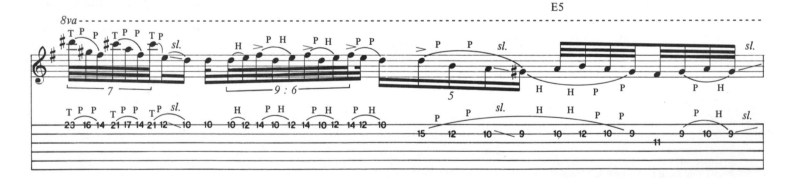

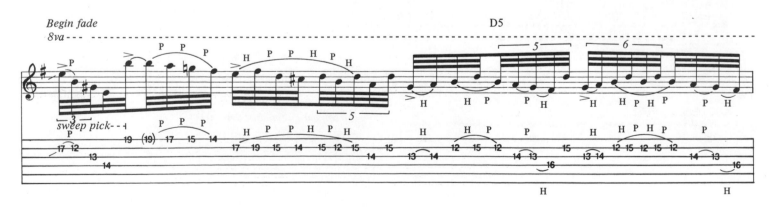

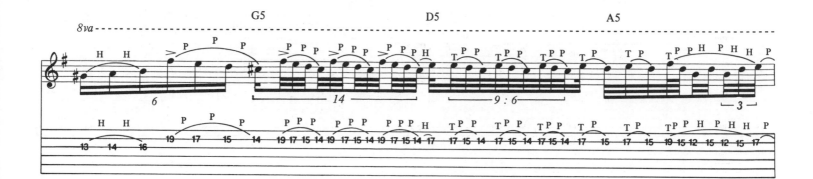

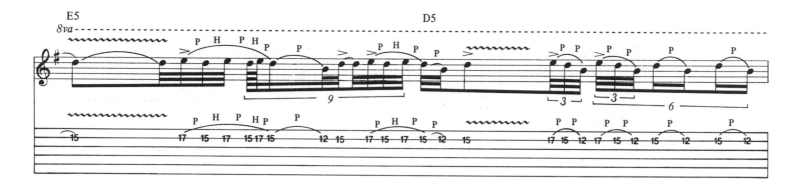

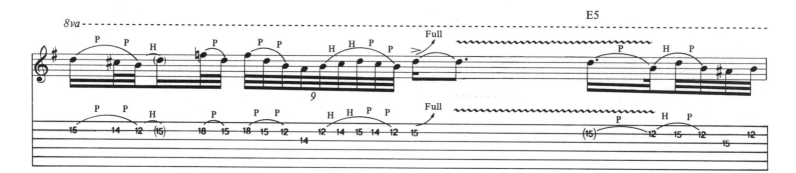

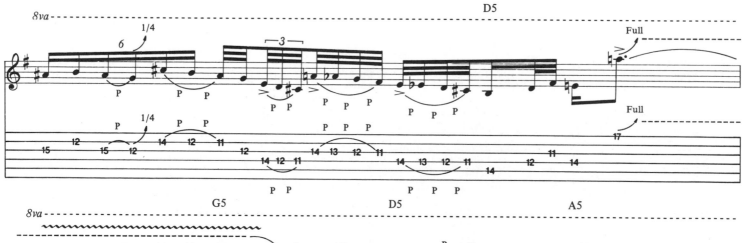

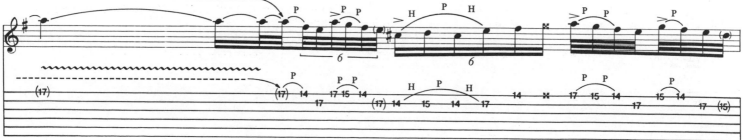

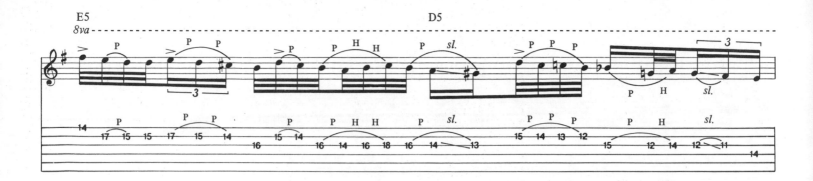

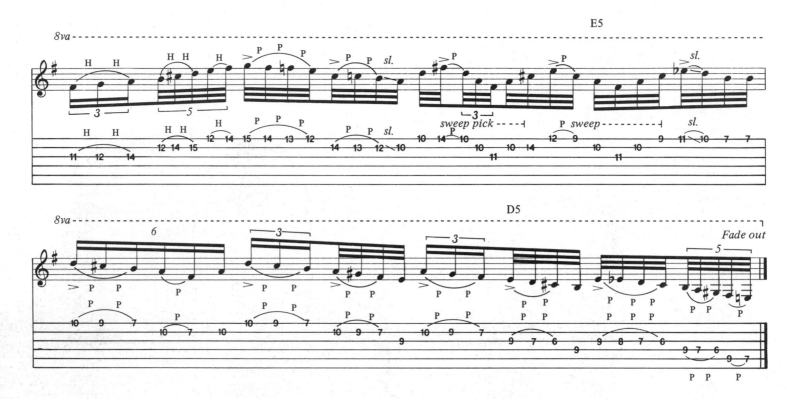

Additional Lyrics

2. Tough girls never break their cool,
   Rough boys know they're the ones who rule.
   I wanna lick your fire, burn you inside.
   Live the sin, inject me in; pleasure, whip me blind.
   Shoot U full of love. *(To Pre-chorus)*

Outro: Shoot U full of love.
   Full of my love.
   Shoot U full of love, love, love, love.

Jay David Buchsbaum

CATHOUSE
As recorded by FASTER PUSSYCAT

Words and Music by
Taime Downe

w/Rhy. Fig. 2 *(3 times)*
G5 .... C ....

Rev up my Chev-y, I'm gon-na pay to play. With a
Per-ver-sion is an a-ver-sion that won't go a-way. I'm a

G5 .... C ....

lick-it-y split___ I like___ that taste,___ I push a-head and fall be-hind.___
hard, hard act___ to swal-low, and she's my bur-ied treas-ure.

G5 .... w/Fill 1
C ....

And such a good, good time,___ we just wan-na stay.
It-'ll be a long, long time___ be-fore I'm on my way.

Chorus
G5 .... D5 .... C5 w/Fill 2

Just got back from the best cat-house___ in town,___ and had the

Rhy. Fig. 3 .... (end Rhy. Fig. 3)

```
-------------------|--7--(7)-7--9-7-7--9--|--5--(5)-5--7-5-5--7--5--|--(5)-5--7-5-5--7--|
-5--5-7-5-5-7------|--5--(5)-5--5-5-5--5--|--3--(3)-3--3-3-3--3--3--|--(3)-3--3-3-3--3--|
-3--3-3-3-3-3------|----------------------|-------------------------|-------------------|
```

w/Rhy. Fig. 3 *(3 times)*
G5 .... D5 w/Fill 3 .... C5 ....

best piece of Mo-na Li-sa I___ ev-er found.___ So

Fill 1

```
-----11-------11----11--(11)-11--|
--9------9-------9----------9-----|
```

Fill 2

```
tr~~~~~~~~~~~~~~~~~~
-----------------------8----11--(11)--|
--8--(8)-------------------------------|
```

Fill 3

```
--------5--(5)-3----5-------5--(5)-3----5------|
--------5--(5)------5-------5--(5)------5------|
--------------5------------------5------------|
```

103

SMASH ALLEY

As recorded by FASTER PUSSYCAT

Words and Music by
Taime Downe and Brent Muscat

Additional Lyrics

2. Captain Friendly locked me in his cage.
He said, "Boys, you'd better behave.
She's only fourteen, in the seventh grade.
If her daddy only knew he'd be screamin' in his grave."
Molested and arrested in Smash Alley. *(To Chorus)*

3. You see, Missy just made it out on parole.
She's huddled in the gutter and she's shivering with cold.
She's so high strung, I'm on the tip of her tongue,
Kneeling in the alley all covered with scum.
Molested and arrested in Smash Alley. *(To Chorus)*

SPEND A YEAR WITH

Eddie Van Halen
Steve Vai
Randy Rhoads
Yngwie Malmsteen
Jimi Hendrix
Vinnie Moore
Stevie Ray Vaughan
Guns N' Roses
Jeff Watson
Carlos Santana
Neal Schon
Eric Clapton
Jimmy Page
Jake E. Lee
Brad Gillis
George Lynch
Metallica
Keith Richards
Jeff Beck
Michael Schenker ...

and save $10.50 off the newsstand price!

Just $24.90 buys you a subscription to GUITAR MAGAZINE and the chance to spend a year studying the techniques and the artistry of the world's best guitar performers.

Every issue of GUITAR gives you:

- sheet music you can't get anywhere else—with accurate transcriptions of the original artists.
- in-depth interviews with guitar greats who candidly discuss the nuts and bolts of what they do.
- columns and articles on the music, the equipment and the techniques that are making waves.

Become a better guitar player and performer. Study with the professionals every month in GUITAR FOR THE PRACTICING MUSICIAN.

To start your subscription—and save 30% off the cover price—write to GUITAR, Box 889, Farmingdale, NY 11737-9789.

Cherry Lane Music Company, Inc.
"quality in printed music"
P.O. Box 430, Port Chester, NY 10573-430